Plastics

Plastics are among the materials that have done most to shape our modern way of life. Just look around your home; in almost every room you will find things made of plastic. Many of the items that you find would be difficult to make from any other material. Plastic objects were once thought of as cheap and inferior, but today a wide range of high-quality products are made from plastics. This book looks in some detail at the nature of plastics, how they are made, and the various kinds of plastic products available in the modern world. Mark Lambert is a freelance author and editor who specializes in science and technology.

DISCARDED

Spotlight on
PLASTICS

Mark Lambert

ROURKE ENTERPRISES INC.
Vero Beach, Florida 32964

Frontispiece *The* Apollo II *command module protected by a sheet of polyethylene.*
Cover *A racing sailboard with sails made of polyester film and polyester fibers.*

Text © 1988 Rourke Enterprises Inc.
PO Box 3328, Vero Beach, Florida 32964

All right reserved. No part of this book may be reproduced or utilized in any form or by any means electronic or mechanical including photocopying, recording or by any information storage and retrieval system without permission in writing from the publishers.

Printed in Italy by G. Canale & C.S.p.A., Turin

Library of Congress Cataloging-in- Publication Data

Lambert, Mark, 1946–
    Spotlight on plastics/Mark Lambert.
      p. cm. – (Spotlight on resources)
    Bibliography: p.
    Includes index.
    Summary: Describes the composition of plastics, the developmental history of this field, and kinds and uses of plastic materials.
    ISBN 0–86592–269–1
    1. Plastics – Juvenile literature.   [1. Plastics.]   I. Title.
II. Series.
TP1125.L36 1988
668.4 – dc 19   87–38304
                                                      CIP
                                                       AC

Contents

1. The plastics revolution — 6
2. The first plastics — 8
3. Carbon chemicals — 10
4. Polymers – long chain molecules — 12
5. Oil to polyethylene — 14
6. Plastics from oil — 16
7. Types of plastics — 18
8. Shaping plastics — 20
9. Plastic fibers — 22
10. Plastic sheets and films — 24
11. Plastic foams — 26
12. Paints and coatings — 28
13. Plastic glues — 30
14. Elastic plastics — 32
15. Plastic mixtures — 34
16. Reinforced plastics — 36
17. The uses of plastics — 38
18. Plastics and the environment — 40
19. Plastics in the future — 42

Appendix: Plastics and their uses — 44
Glossary — 46
Index — 47

1. The plastics revolution

For thousands of years traditional materials for making everyday objects have included such things as wood, clay and metal. Plastics, on the other hand, have been in use for less than 130 years and most of them have been developed within the last thirty years. But despite their short history they are now one of our most important materials. Plastics are used to make many of the everyday objects that we use in our homes, such as kitchen utensils, bathroom fittings, clothing, toothbrushes, food wrappings and toys, to name but a few.

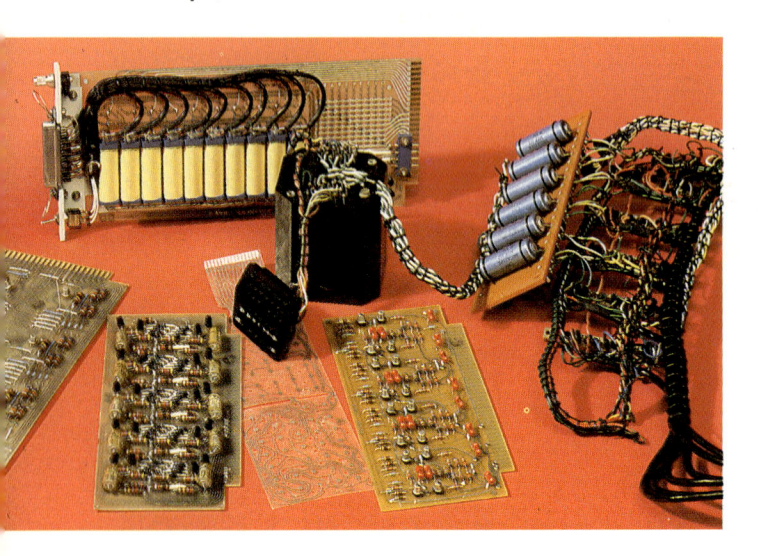

Although it looks like glass, this ornament is actually made of polystyrene.

Because they are such good insulators, plastics are essential to the electronics industry.

Plastics are extremely good electrical insulators (that is, electric currents cannot pass through them) and so various kinds of plastics are important components of light and power switches, televisions, radios and computers. Plastics are particularly resistant to corrosion and to attack by strong chemicals. Many plastics also have special properties, such as strength, flexibility or slipperiness.

But what are plastics? When we describe something as being plastic, we mean that it can be molded or formed into any shape. Plasticine is a good example of this. On the other hand, we have come to use the word plastic to describe a range of materials that are often hard and inflexible. It is true that these materials can all, at some stage, be molded by applying heat and pressure. But so too can glass and many metals. What makes plastics different is that their molecules are based on carbon atoms. And these are arranged in long chains.

Plastics are also referred to as resins. This is because they have properties similar to those of natural plant resins – substances known to scientists long before the invention of plastics.

Colorful plastics are now common in most homes.

2. The first plastics

The history of plastic goes back over a hundred years. The first plastic was produced in 1862 by Alexander Parkes, an English chemist, using a chemical called cellulose nitrate. This chemical was made from plant cellulose – the material that makes up the cell walls of plants. By itself cellulose nitrate is hard and brittle, but Parkes discovered that by adding camphor he could turn it into an ivory-like material that could be softened and molded. He called it Parkesine, but although he won awards for this new material, it was never widely used.

Bakelite rapidly became popular for use in electrical equipment.

The discovery of celluloid was vital to the development of the film industry.

In contrast, the next plastic to appear was an enormous success. In 1869 John W. Hyatt, an American printer, developed a material similar to Parkesine, which he named celluloid. He had been looking for material for making billiard balls, and at first celluloid was regarded as a substitute for ivory and tortoiseshell. But celluloid was soon being used to make such things as toys and car windshields. Later it became vital to the development of the film industry and today it is still used to make ping-pong balls.

In 1897 some German chemists found that casein, a chemical found in milk, could be treated to produce another kind of plastic. This was cheaper to make than celluloid, but it was a slow process. Then in 1910 Henry Baekland, an American chemist, produced the first completely synthetic plastic, which he called Bakelite. This was soon being widely used as an electrical insulator and to manufacture such things as door handles, telephones and the handles of kitchen implements.

In the 1920s the first phonograph records were made of Bakelite.

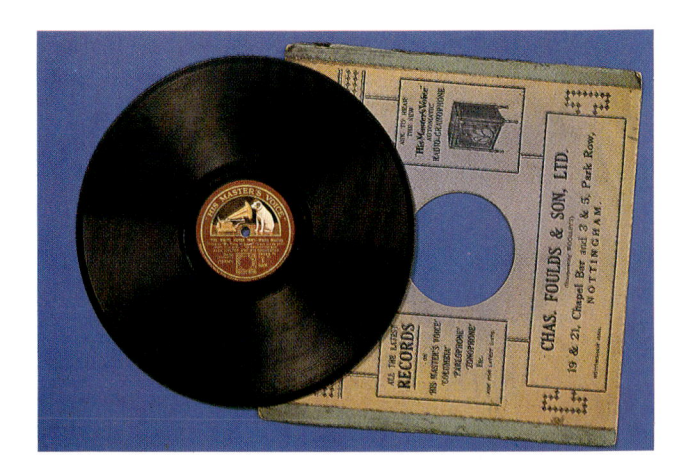

Below *These 1920s dolls were made of celluloid.*

3. Carbon chemicals

All plastics, like these acrylic blocks, are based on molecules containing carbon atoms.

All matter is made up of tiny particles called atoms. A substance that consists entirely of identical atoms is called an element. There are over a hundred different elements, ninety-two of which occur naturally. Examples include hydrogen, iron, silver, nitrogen and chlorine. Very often atoms of the same or different elements bond together to form structures known as molecules. Substances whose molecules contain atoms of more than one element are called compounds. For example, hydrogen and chlorine atoms can bond together to form the compound hydrogen chloride.

One of the most common elements is carbon. In fact it is so common that an entirely separate branch of chemistry is devoted to carbon compounds. Carbon-based chemicals are often known as organic chemicals, because they were first discovered in living organisms. Only later did scientists realize that the chemical processes that occur inside living cells are essentially the same as those that also take place in non-living materials.

Carbon combines easily with many other elements, the most common compounds being those of carbon and hydrogen. The simplest of such compounds is methane gas, whose molecules contain just one carbon atom with four hydrogen atoms. Ethane has two carbon atoms and six hydrogen atoms. The gas ethylene, on the other hand, has two carbon atoms and only four hydrogen atoms. Each carbon atom is linked to two rather than three hydrogen atoms and it shares the "spare" bond with the other carbon atom, forming a double bond. Compounds with such double bonds react easily and are the basis of many plastics.

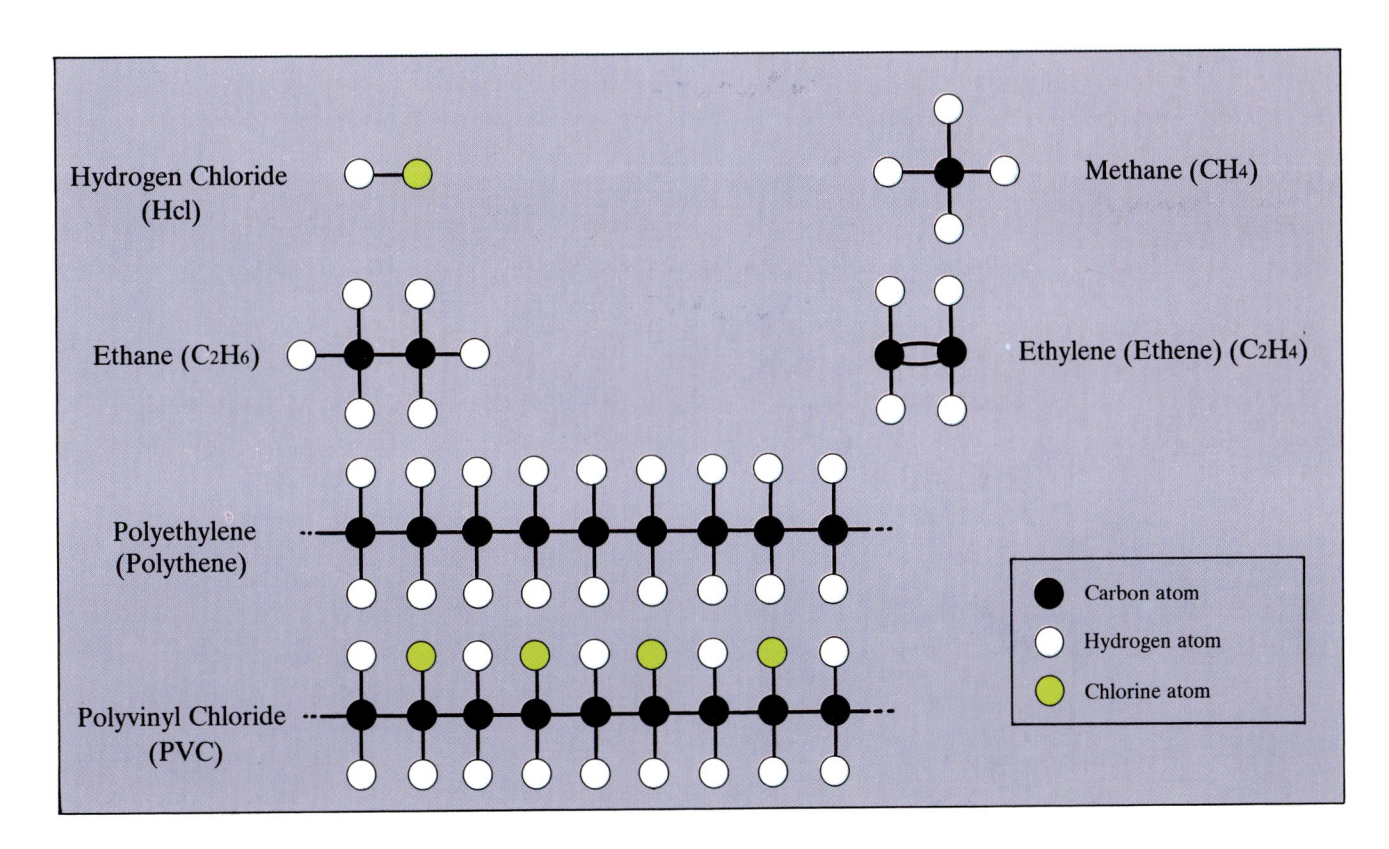

Some chemical compounds and their molecular structure.

4. Polymers – long chain molecules

The molecules of a number of carbon-based compounds consist of long chains, made up from many repeating sub-units. The sub-units are known as monomers and the long chains are called polymers. Some polymers occur naturally; examples include plant cellulose and isoprene, the polymer in rubber. However, many polymers can be created artificially. Synthetic polymers are what we know as plastics.

The process of creating long chain molecules from monomers is called polymerization. There are two ways in which this process can take place. The first is called addition polymerization, when the monomers simply join together. For example, when ethylene gas is heated to a high temperature under pressure, the double bonds between the carbon atoms break down and the ethylene monomers join up to form

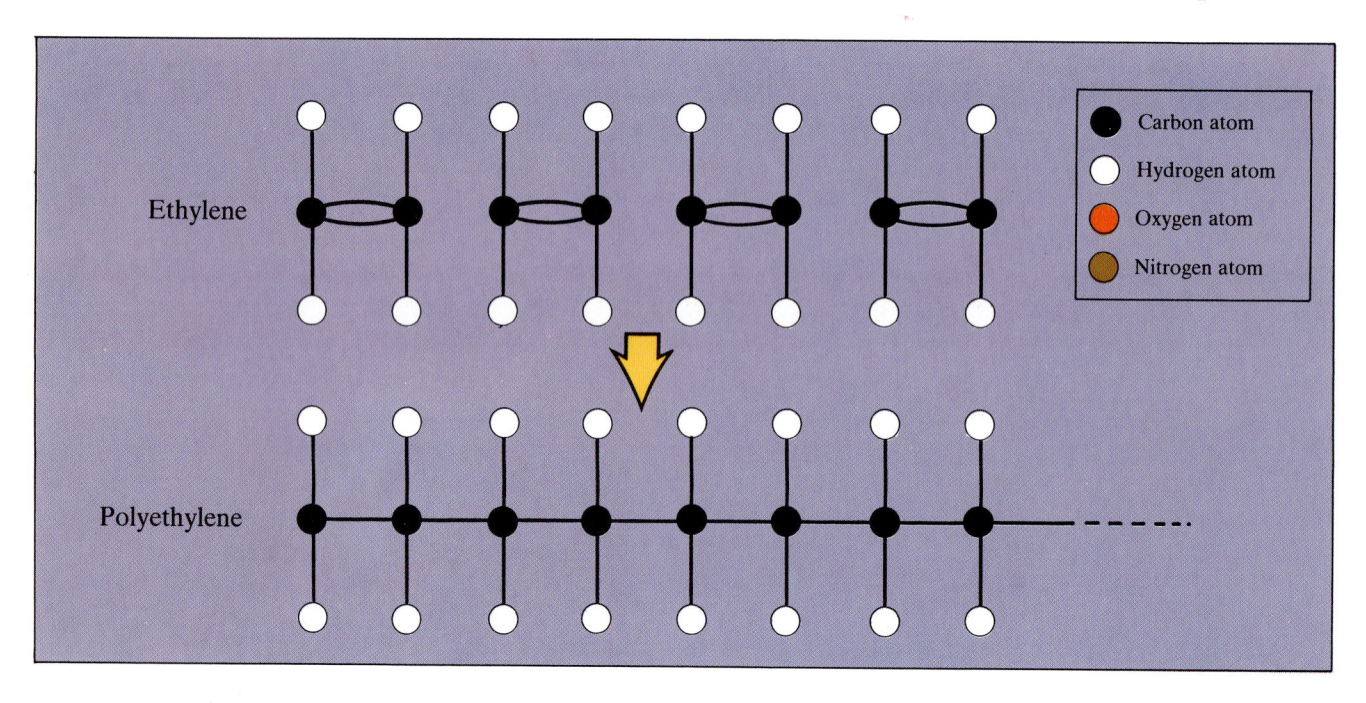

In addition polymerization, a number of monomer molecules join up to form a polymer.

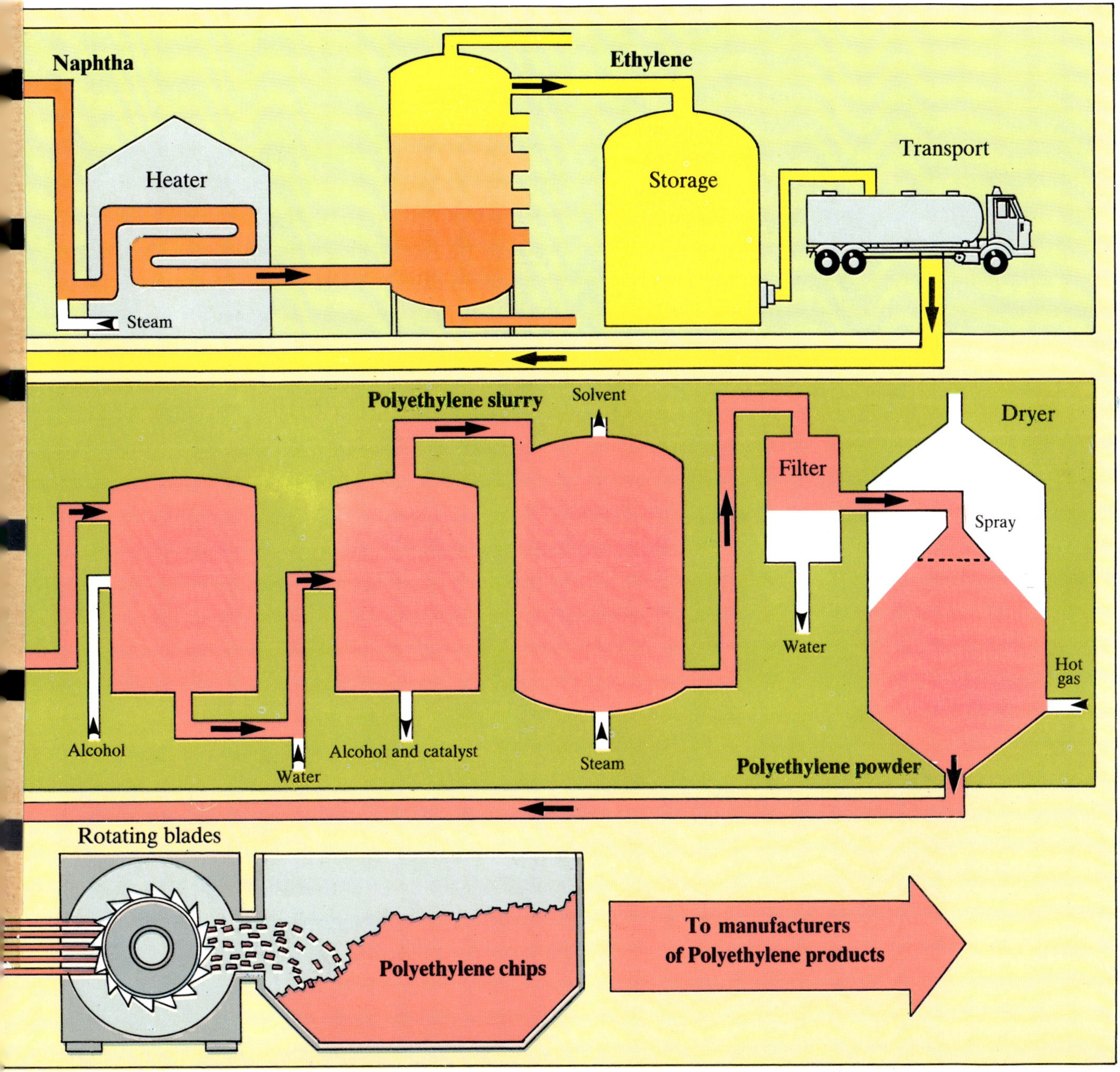
Naphtha
Ethylene
Heater
Storage
Transport
Steam
Polyethylene slurry
Solvent
Dryer
Filter
Spray
Water
Hot gas
Alcohol
Water
Alcohol and catalyst
Steam
Polyethylene powder
Rotating blades
Polyethylene chips
To manufacturers of Polyethylene products

6. Plastics from oil

Almost all plastics are made from organic (carbon-based) chemicals. When plastics were first discovered, such chemicals could only be obtained in fairly small amounts from coal tar. But during the 1930s several important things happened. First, techniques for refining crude oil were improving rapidly and chemists were beginning to realize that oil contained many useful organic chemicals. Meanwhile, in 1935, William Carothers, an American chemist, had succeeded in making nylon. The obvious usefulness of this material led chemists to take an increasing interest in plastics.

At a refinery crude oil is separated into mixtures of chemicals by distilling it in a fractionating tower. The oil is heated so that its various

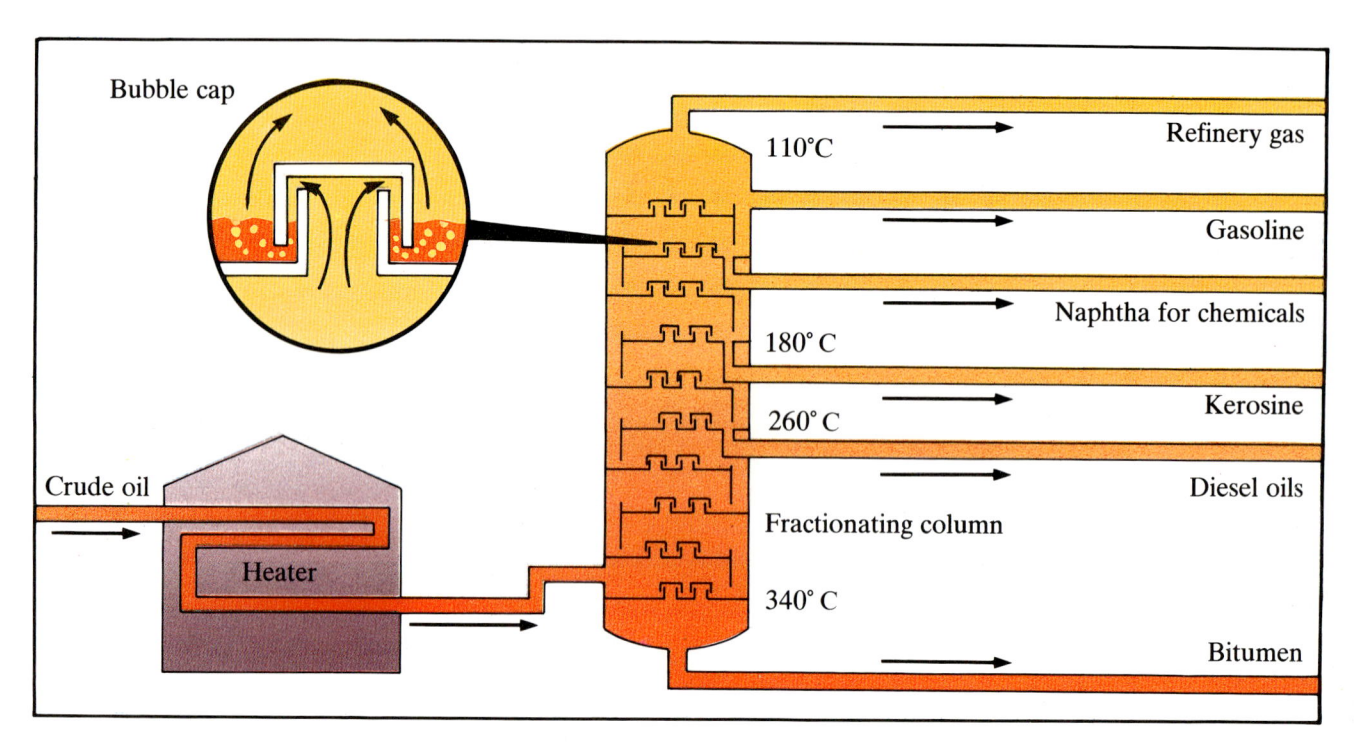

Naphtha is one of several by-products produced by heating crude oil in a fractionating tower.

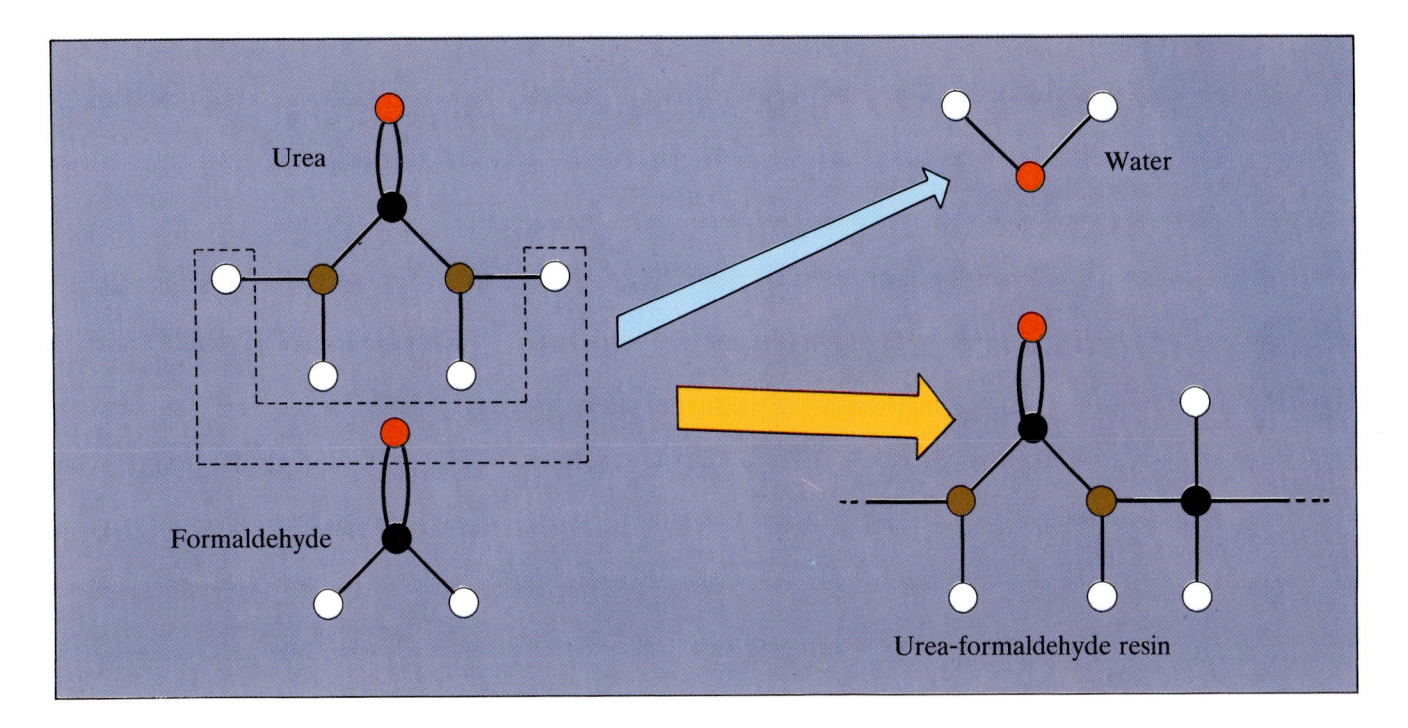

long chains. The end product is a solid plastic called polyethylene. Other polymers made by addition polymerization include polypropylene, polyvinyl chloride (PVC), polystyrene, Perspex and polytetrafluoroethylene (PTFE), the chemical-resistant, nonstick plastic often known by such trade names as Teflon and Fluon.

The other way this process can take place is known as condensation polymerization. In most cases two chemicals are made to react together and the long chain molecules of the resulting polymer therefore consist of two alternating monomers. As the monomers join together, a condensation by-product, such as water or hydrogen chloride, is formed. Poly-

In condensation polymerization, a polymer is formed from two different monomers. At the same time, condensate is given off.

mers formed by condensation reactions include polyesters, polycarbonates, polyurethanes and nylons.

Below *Polypropylene helmets.*

5. Oil to polyethylene

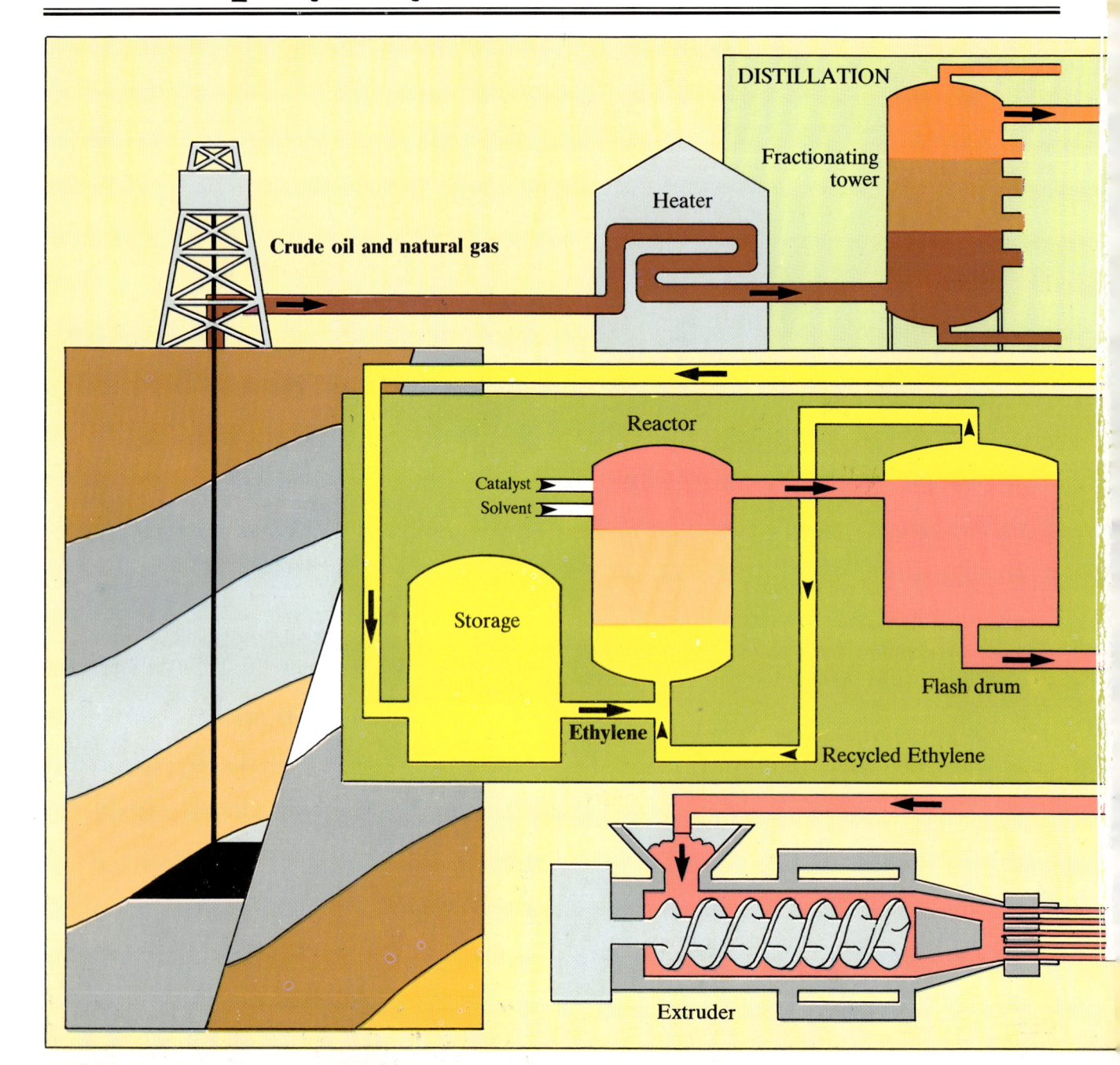

chemicals boil and vaporize. The heaviest fractions with the highest boiling points condense (become liquid again) low down in the tower and are removed. A mixture of light gases known as naphtha reaches a level near the top of the tower and this too is piped away. One of the gases contained in naphtha is ethylene, which is used not only to make polyethythene but also to manufacture a number of other plastics, such as polyvinyl chloride (PVC), polyvinyl acetate, polystyrene and acrylics.

Other important chemicals obtained from crude oil include propylene, butylene, benzene and methyl alcohol. Natural gas also contains some of these chemicals. Today, oil and natural gas are vital sources of the chemicals used in the plastics industry.

Today, nylon has a variety of uses, such as sealing rings (**above**) *and the casing for an electrode used to monitor an unborn baby* (**below**).

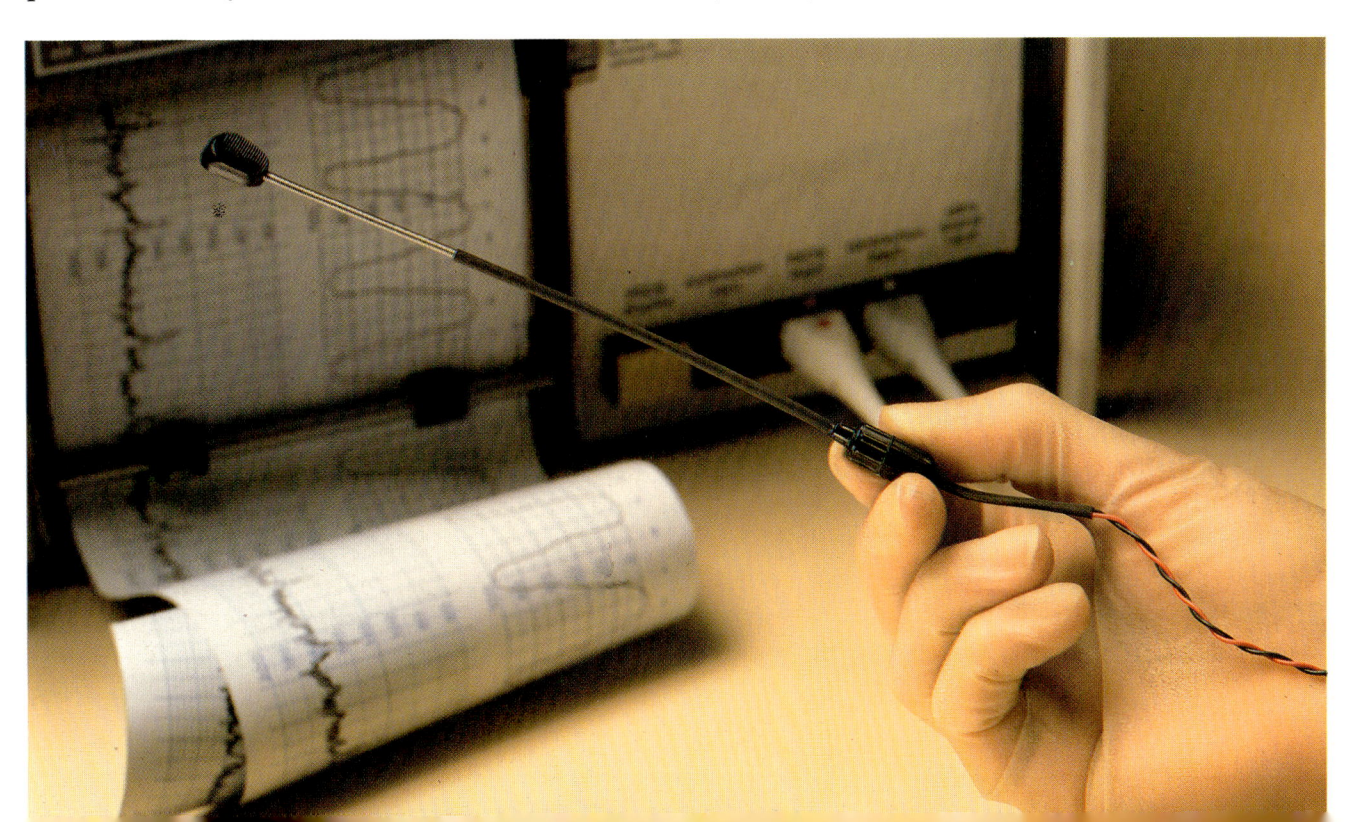

7. Types of plastics

Molecules in a thermosoftening plastic **(left)** *and a thermosetting plastic* **(right)**.

Plastics are divided into two main types – thermosoftening and thermosetting. These names refer to what happens when plastic materials are subjected to heat ("thermo" comes from the Greek word meaning heat).

Thermosoftening plastics become soft and pliable when they are heated and harden again when cooled. This process can be repeated again and again. Among the many thermosoftening plastics are polyethythene, polypropylene, polystyrene, PVC, nylon, polycarbonate, acrylics and PTFE. Some of these soften at fairly low temperatures, but others can withstand considerable heat. For example, in boiling water polyethylene becomes soft and easily deformed, but nylon keeps its shape. And a coating of the nonstick plastic PTFE is unaffected by the heat of a frying pan.

When a thermosoftening plastic is heated, its long chain molecules become flexible and move freely in relation to each other. This is what makes it possible to mold such a plastic again and again. A thermosetting plastic, on the other hand, can be molded only once – during

Above *Thermosoftening and thermosetting plastics are used to make thermos flasks.*

the polymerization stage of its manufacture. This is because chemical reactions take place when the plastic is heated. Cross-links form between the long chain molecules, which thus form a three-dimensional network. Heating the plastic only causes more cross-links to form and the plastic becomes harder. Thermosetting plastics include phenol-formaldehyde (Bakelite), polyurethanes, polyester resins and epoxy resins. Thermosetting plastics are not as easy to manufacture as thermosoftening kinds, but they are useful for manufacturing heat-resistant objects, such as light fittings, saucepan handles and kitchen work surfaces.

Thermosetting plastics are used to make a wide range of tough, heat-resistant articles.

19

8. Shaping plastics

There are many ways in which plastic objects can be manufactured. Some items are made by a process called extrusion. Hot plastic is squeezed through a specially shaped hole to produce a long piece of plastic that has the same cross section throughout its length. Extrusion is used to produce water pipes, curtain tracks and thick plastic sheets.

Many plastic objects are produced by molding, of which there are several methods. In injection molding, hot plastic is forced into a mold. This is then cooled and opened to remove the solid plastic object inside. In blow molding, a hot plastic tube is pushed between the two halves of a mold. The mold is then closed and air is blown into the tube, causing it to take up the shape of the inside of the mold. Plastic bottles, toys and many other hollow objects are made by this method.

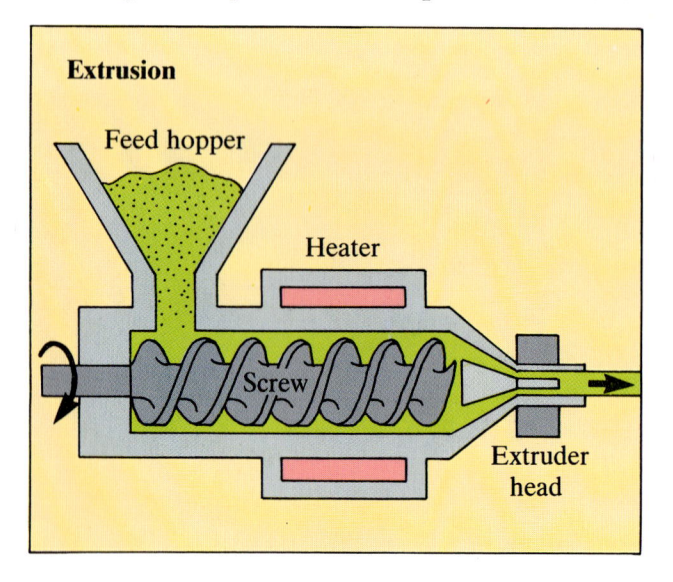

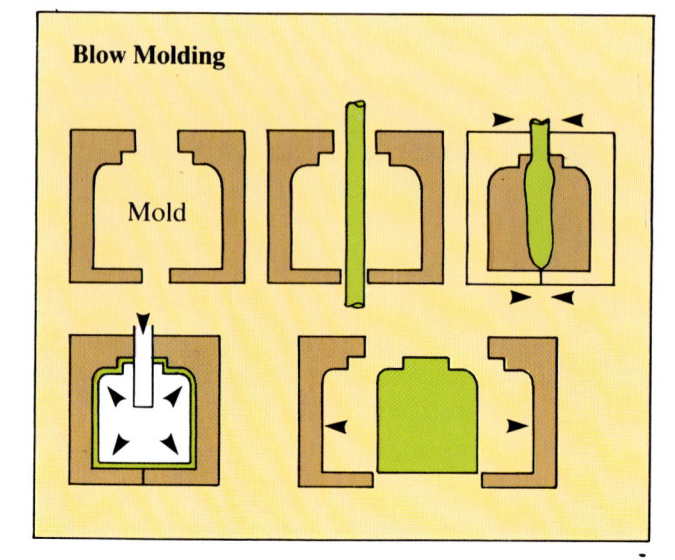

Another molding technique is known as vacuum forming. In this method plastic sheet is held in a frame, heated and then drawn onto a mold by suction. Boat hulls, refrigerator linings, egg boxes and acrylic bathtubs are made by vacuum forming. In compression molding, powdered plastic is placed in a mold, heated and then squeezed into shape by the two halves of the mold. Plastic bottle tops and toilet seats are made in this way.

Large thick-walled items, such as garbage cans and water tanks, are made by a process called rotational molding. In this process powdered plastic is melted and tumbled inside a rotating mold and allowed to form a skin inside the mold. Yet another technique for forming plastics is known as calendering. This is done on large heated rollers and produces thin plastic sheets or films.

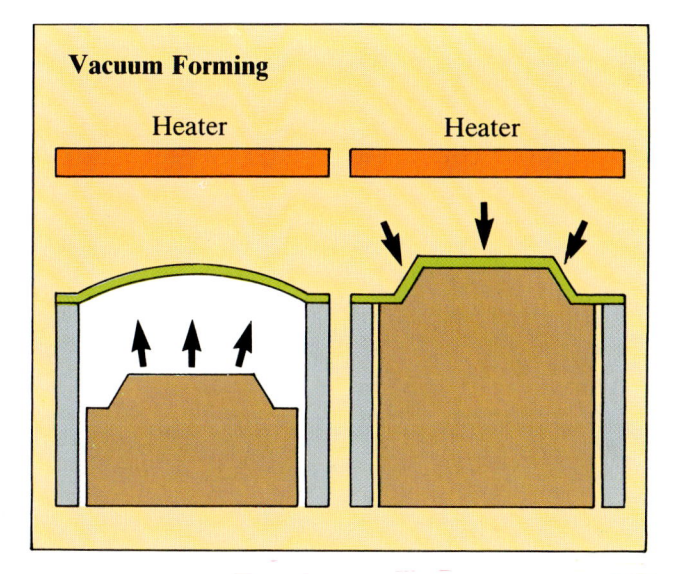

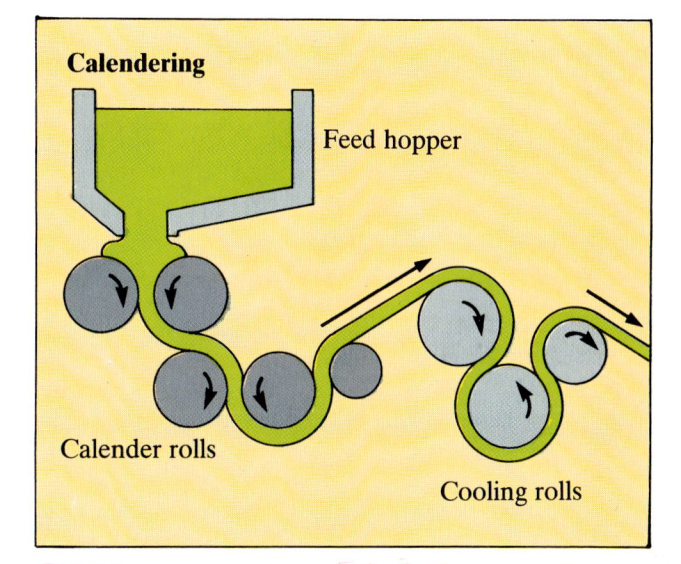

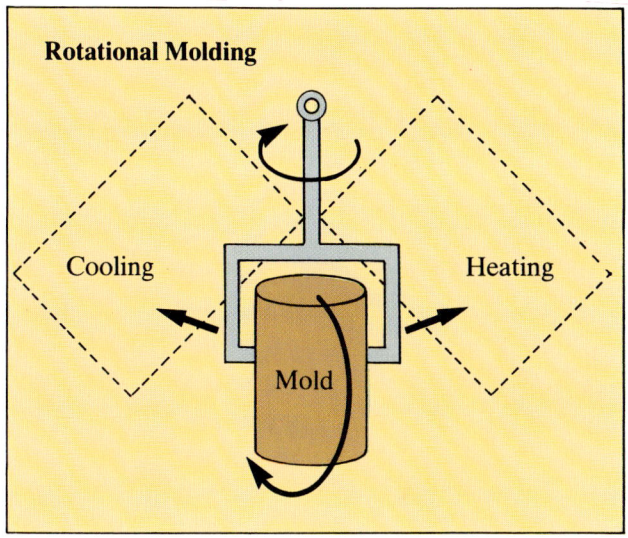

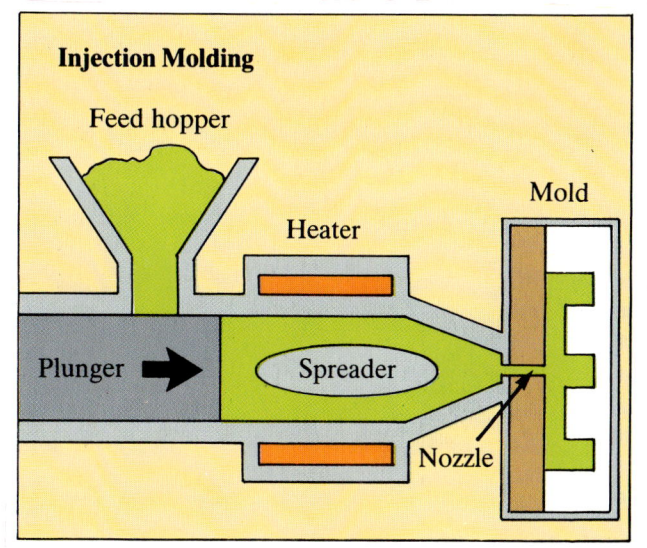

9. Plastic fibers

The long chain molecules of plastics can easily be drawn out into long thin fibers. Synthetic fibers are made, or spun, by forcing a polymer material through tiny holes, or spinnarets. The hot fibers are then stretched to help align the molecules alongside each other and strengthen the finished fibers.

Synthetic fibers were first discovered over a hundred years ago. At that time the only fibers available for making fabrics were natural ones, such as wool, cotton and silk. Silk is a cellulose fiber made by silk moth caterpillars from plant

The fire-resistant clothes worn by racing drivers are made of synthetic material.

cellulose. It is a delicate, much sought after and expensive fiber, and during the 1880s people began looking for ways of artificially producing it. In 1889 Count Hilaire de Chardonnet succeeded, producing an artificial silk made from cellulose nitrate derived from plant cellulose. Cellulose nitrate is highly flammable, however, so Chardonnet silk was later made from pure cellulose. Chardonnet's process has since been replaced by cheaper, more efficient ones. Modern artificial silks are known as cuprammonium and viscose rayons.

People who work in the food industry need hardwearing clothes that are easy to clean.

During the early 1900s scientists began to look for ways of producing completely synthetic fibers. In the United States in 1935 a group of chemists directed by Wallace H. Carothers produced the first commercially successful fiber, known as nylon. Since then many other polymer fibers have been developed. Important modern textile fibers include acetate rayons (cellulose acetate), polyesters, polyurethanes, polyacrylonitrile and polypropylene.

Synthetic fibers can resemble natural fibers, but they have special properties, such as crease-resistance.

10. Plastic sheets and films

Plastics are often manufactured in the form of flat sheets, which can then be worked to produce a variety of different shapes. A sheet may be made by casting it in a mold, or it may be extruded through a long, narrow slit. Among the plastics most commonly formed in sheets are polyethythene, PVC and acrylics, often known as Perspex.

Perspex canopies on Dutch canal boats.

One of the most important properties of Perspex is its transparency, and its wide variety of uses include cockpit canopies for aircraft, secondary double glazing in homes and light fittings. Another transparent plastic is polycarbonate, which is much stronger than Perspex and is used to make bulletproof glazing, riot shields and baby bottles. It can also be made opaque by adding colors and fillers and is then used to make safety helmets, unbreakable crockery, telephones and electrical sockets.

Thin plastic sheets and films are generally produced by calendering. Softened plastic is fed into a series of large heated rollers, which squeeze it flat before it is cooled. Very thin films are produced by using cold air to expand thin tubing that has just been extruded. Thin plastic sheeting has a wide range of uses. For example, polyethythene is used as a dampproof membrane underneath new buildings and to make such things as silage coverings, fertilizer sacks and shopping bags. Clear polyethythene is used to make food storage bags. Very thin plastic film is used to "shrink wrap" food.

Polyethythene is used underneath the floors of many new buildings to keep out damp.

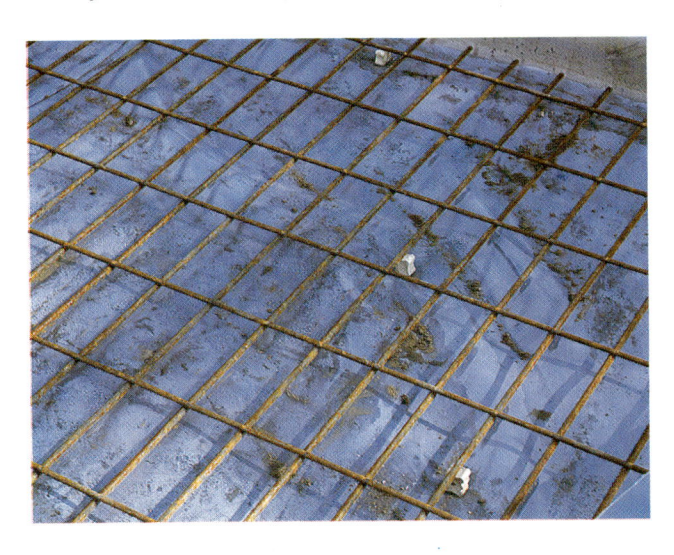

Below *Polyethythene used as a mulch for strawberries. This keeps the weeds down and protects the fruit.*

11. Plastic foams

Several plastics can be manufactured in the form of foams. These are made by producing bubbles of gas in a molten plastic. The plastic therefore expands and, as it cools and becomes solid, the gas bubbles become trapped. The gas can be introduced into the plastic in a variety of ways. It can be produced as a result of a chemical reaction, or it can be generated by causing a liquid to vaporize. It can also be produced by simply whipping the liquid plastic or blowing gas through it.

Among the most commonly foamed plastics are polyurethanes. These are often produced in the form of structural foam — slabs of rigid foam with a hard, smooth outer skin. This type of foam can be produced by injection molding to make lightweight furniture parts. Rigid foams for the building industry are often made sandwiched between sheets of wood, plaster-

Polystyrene foam used as an insulating material in the building industry.

board or metal. Another thermosetting resin commonly used in the form of a foam is urea-formaldehyde. This is often injected into the cavity walls of houses to provide insulation.

Polyurethanes can also be used to make flexible foams for use in furniture. The main disadvantage of this material is that it produces poisonous, choking fumes if it catches fire.

Another common foam is expanded polystyrene. This is usually made in the form of beads, which are then molded to any shape. Expanded polystyrene is used for packing delicate items, as an insulation and soundproofing material and to make inexpensive cups, pots and dishes. Other foams include plasticized PVC foam, used in upholstery, and polyethylene foam, used for insulating electric cables.

Under the microscope polyethylene foam can be seen to consist of bubbles of air.

12. Paints and coatings

A huge coated-nylon warehouse. The fabric, woven from nylon and coated with PVC, is completely waterproof and very strong. It is held up by air pumped from fans.

Plastics resist corrosion and attack by chemicals and this makes them very suitable as protective coatings. These can be applied in several different ways. A sheet of metal can be coated by simply gluing a thin film of plastic to the surface. Metal objects with more complicated shapes can be dipped in molten plastic. Alternatively, a metal object can be heated and then immersed in finely powdered plastic. The plastic touching the surface melts and sticks to the metal. Yet another method involves using an electrostatic spray gun to spray electrically

Many modern paints contain plastics to give a hard-wearing finish.

charged particles of plastic onto an earthed (connected to the ground) metal object. The plastic particles stick evenly to the object. This is then placed in a hot oven to melt the plastic, which then forms an even coating.

Paper is often coated with plastic to make it waterproof, hard-wearing or attractive – the cover of this book has a plastic coating produced using rollers to press a layer of hot, extruded polyethythene to the paper. Fabrics can be coated with plastic (usually PVC) in the form of a paste, which is spread evenly and then cured by heat. Coated fabrics are used in clothing, car seats and washable vinyl wallpapers.

Plastics have also become common ingredients of modern paints. They have replaced natural resins that were used formerly. Polyvinyl acetate is commonly used in water-based, emulsion paints. Thermosetting resins, such as polyurethanes, melamine-formaldehyde and epoxy resins are used in gloss paints and provide a very hard-wearing finish.

13. Plastic glues

A solid plastic object may, at first, seem far removed from the sticky materials we know as glues. But in fact many plastics can be made sticky, by either melting them or dissolving them in suitable liquids, or solvents. And when suitably treated, some plastics make very efficient glues.

Polyvinyl acetate glue being used to fix a joint in a wooden chair.

A close-up of the adhesive "tack" of a polymer adhesive.

Some glues are made using thermoplastic resins. Commonly used solvent-based polymer adhesives include such things as polystyrene cement and polychloroprene (neoprene) rubber solution. A solution of polyvinyl acetate is also sometimes used as a glue.

Thermosetting resins are used to make reactive adhesives. One of the best known of these is sold under the name Araldite. It consists of an epoxy resin and a separate hardener, and when the two are mixed, a chemical reaction takes place and the hard resin that forms bonds firmly to most types of surfaces. Another variation is known as an epoxy film adhesive. A film of material is placed between the parts to be joined. Pressure and heat are then applied and the film first melts and then sets.

Some other reactive adhesives include urea-formaldehyde, which is used to bond layers of plywood together, and resorcinal-formaldehyde, which is used to produce very water-resistant bonds in wood. An acrylic glue consists of a resin and a separate catalyst, each of which are applied to different surfaces. When these are brought together, the resin rapidly polymerizes and sets hard. A "superglue" is made from a monomer, usually ethyl cyanoacrylate. Inside the tube this is kept liquid by a special chemical. But when the glue is applied to a surface, tiny amounts of water "overpower" the stabilizing chemical and polymerization takes place. Superglue sprays are being developed for use in an emergency or on battlefields to help close up deep wounds.

Paper being treated with a preparation of thermosetting resins to produce a laminate.

14. Elastic plastics

A racing car's tires must be reliable under all conditions. High-quality tires contain styrene/butadiene rubber.

Rubber contains a natural polymer with one very important property. If it is stretched and then released, it returns to its original shape. This elasticity is due to the fact that the long chain molecules are not straight but twisted up into a tangle. When the molecules are pulled, they straighten out, but return to their tangled state when released again.

The rubber polymer, isoprene, can be made artificially, but man-made polyisoprene is more expensive than natural rubber. The chemical chloroprene is very similar to isoprene and polychloroprene (neoprene) is a synthetic rubber used to make strong, oil-resistant hoses and gaskets. Other synthetic chemicals with properties close to those of isoprene are butadiene and styrene, both of which are manufactured using oil chemicals. These monomers are combined to make the polymer known as SBR (styrene/butadiene rubber), which is used in the manufacture of car tires, hoses, shoe soles and waterproof boots.

Butadiene is also used to make other artificial rubbers. For example, the polymer of butadiene and acrylonitrile is known as nitrile rubber, which is very resistant to chemical attack. It is used to make oil seals and flexible fuel tanks.

Silicone rubbers are unusual polymers in that their long chain molecules are not based on carbon atoms. Instead, they consist of alternating silicon and oxygen atoms. Silicone rubbers are less strong than natural rubber, but they repel water and are very resistant to both heat and chemical attack. Silicones are also made in the form of liquids and solid resins.

An elastomer is used to create a life-like "rubber" mask for a theatrical production.

15. Plastic mixtures

Many plastic materials are made by polymerizing one kind of monomer. But it is possible to combine the useful properties of two or more plastics in a single material known as a copolymer, made by polymerizing two or more monomers together. And by varying the proportions in which the monomers are mixed, it is possible to produce a whole range of plastics with different properties.

One example of a copolymer is vinyl chloride/vinyl acetate, which is used to make phonograph records and rigid clear sheeting. Ethylene/vinyl acetate (EVA) is a very flexible, easily sealed copolymer used extensively by the food industry as an alternative to

Plasticizer can be added to PVC in varying amounts to make it more flexible.

polyethylene. Acrylonitrile/butadiene/styrene has a number of important properties, such as resistance to impact and scuffing, and is therefore used to make luggage, refrigerator linings and food containers. Acrylonitrile/vinyl acetate is made into a fiber and sold as Acrilan.

In many cases the properties of plastics can be improved by adding other substances. For example, graphite and molybdenum disulfide both increase the slipperiness of a plastic. Special plasticizers are used to make plastics more flexible, and other substances can be added to make plastics more resistant to the effects of heat and light.

A telephone made of acrylonitrile/butadiene/styrene, a tough, impact-resistant mixture.

Heat-resistant plastics are extensively used in the aerospace industry.

Plastics can also be mixed with other materials. For example, paper towels and handkerchieves are given extra wet strength by adding a small amount of urea-formaldehyde resin to the pulp from which the paper is made. When the paper is dried by heating, the resin sets and holds the fibers together even when they are wetted again. Urea-formaldehyde resin is also used to produce crease-resistant cotton fabric. And melamine-formaldehyde resin is used to help preserve waterproofing and other special finishes in cotton.

16. Reinforced plastics

One of the most important properties of plastics is their lightness, which makes them especially useful in situations where metals would be too heavy. However, plastics are not as strong as metals. But this can be overcome by reinforcing them with other materials.

One of the most common reinforcing materials is glass, in the form of thin fibers woven into a mat or fabric. The thermosetting plastic known as polyester resin is commonly reinforced with glass fibers. This type of glass-reinforced plastic (GRP) is used to make boat hulls, car bodies, furniture, railroad cars and aircraft seats.

Other materials used to reinforce plastics include asbestos, cotton and nylon fiber. Among the strongest reinforced plastics are those made using carbon fibers. These contain long chains of pure carbon and are made by heat-treating polyacrylonitrile (PAN) textile fibers. Reinforced plastics are rigid materials that can be built up to any required thickness or molded to any shape. Once formed, they can be machined in much the same way as metals.

Yet another way of reinforcing plastic is laminating – building up layers of material. Kitchen worktops and table mats are often laminated plastics, made by compressing together layers of paper impregnated with a thermoset-

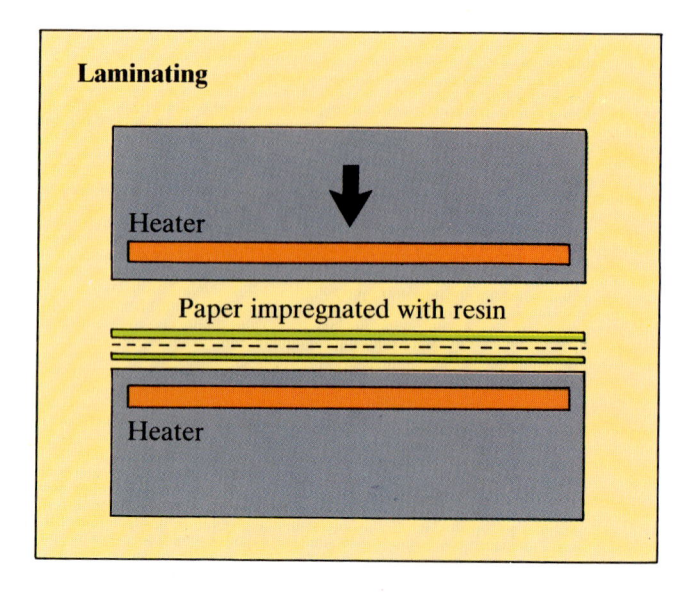

To produce a laminate, layers of paper impregnated with thermosetting resin are compressed together and heated.

ting resin, such as melamine-formaldehyde or Bakelite. Worktops can be made attractive by producing a colored pattern on the upper layer of paper and protecting it with a transparent layer of resin.

In addition to the plastic resin and its reinforcement, a third material, often a metal, can be added. For example, printed circuit boards for use in electronic hardware are made from copper-clad laminates.

The nose cone of Concorde is made of glass-reinforced plastic.

17. The uses of plastics

Polyethylene was discovered accidentally in 1933 by scientists working at Imperial Chemical Industries (ICI) in Britain. But it was not until 1953, when the German chemist Karl Ziegler discovered a greatly improved method for making polyethythene, that it began to be produced in any quantity. Today, polyethythene is a material that we would find very hard to do without.

Plastic has a wide range of uses. Here it is made into a piece of modern jewelry.

These growing bags are made of polyethythene, a commonly used plastic.

In the last thirty years plastics have replaced other materials in a wide range of products. For example, many items that were formerly made from metals, such as steel, iron, aluminum, copper, zinc and brass, are now made form plastics such as polyethythene, polypropylene, nylon, acrylic and acetal. In many products glass has been replaced by polycarbonate and Perspex. Polyester GRP is used in place of wood, brick, concrete and metals. PVC is often used in place of leather, and synthetic fibers are often used instead of natural ones, such as wool, cotton, hemp and sisal.

The plastic with probably the most varied uses is nylon (polyamide). In engineering it is used to make nuts and bolts, bearings and sprockets. In the home it can be found in cupboard hinges, brooms, zip fasteners, shower fittings, washing machine parts, toys and electric switch casings. Glass-reinforced nylon is used to make bicycle wheels, power tool casings and fishing reels. And, of course, nylon is used in the manufacture of a wide range of clothing and furnishing fabrics.

Acrylic, or Perspex, was used to re-glaze the Palm House in Gothenburg, Sweden.

18. Plastics and the environment

A large number of modern plastic products are intended to be disposed of after use – obvious examples include food wrappings and containers. And many other plastic articles are thrown away when they are no longer required. But, unlike paper, plastics decompose only very slowly. And unlike most metals, they do not corrode or rust. The disposal of plastic waste therefore poses many problems.

Most plastics burn easily. However, many plastics give off poisonous or irritating fumes when burned and these add to the problem of air pollution. Alternatively, it is possible to add chemicals to plastics that speed up the process of decomposition. This, to some extent, helps to overcome the problem of plastic litter. But such chemicals do make plastics more expensive to produce and, in any case, disposing of plastic simply by throwing it away seems very wasteful.

Plastic waste is usually mixed with a variety of other materials. The most efficient way to deal with it is to remove noncombustible materials, such as metals and glass, and use the rest as a fuel for generating electricity. Alternatively, some plastic waste can be sorted and recycled. At present, it is possible to recycle polyethythene, PET and acrylic, although only acrylic can be recycled back to its original form.

Plastic waste decomposes very slowly. **Above** *Pollution on the banks of the Thames River, England.*

Nonbiodegradable plastic washed up on the shores of Australia.

19. Plastics in the future

Modern technology progresses at a rapid pace and new uses for plastics are continually being discovered. Among the latest plastics are a group known as polyimides. These are highly resistant both to mechanical wear and to chemicals, and scientists have found uses for them in space shuttles and particle accelerators (huge devices for smashing atoms). Another recently developed plastic, sold under the name Sorbothane, is an elastomer with a remarkable property. When cut, it rapidly heals itself. This makes it especially useful for seals in gas pipes.

Among the latest fibers are a group known as aramids, which were developed from nylons. Unlike most plastics, these fibers do not burn — instead they char like wool. And they are immensely strong. The lightweight fabric kevlar, based on aramid fibers, is used to make bulletproof jackets and protective clothing for chain-saw operators and workers in other dangerous occupations.

The demand for plastics has increased rapidly in recent years and continues to do so. Today, crude oil and natural gas are the main sources of the monomers from which plastics are made. The petrochemical industry consumes many millions of tons of oil each year. In the short term there appears to be plenty of oil available

The space vehicles of the future will rely heavily on plastic components.

and new oil reserves are still being found. But even so, oil supplies cannot last forever. Sometime in the next twenty or thirty years, oil supplies may begin to run out. And even though the necessary chemicals can be obtained from coal, the cost of producing plastics is likely to increase dramatically. Scientists may succeed in devising ways of producing plastics from renewable resources, such as plant chemicals.

This mouse survives underwater in a bag made of a silicone membrane. Oxygen from the water is filtered through the membrane, and the mouse breathes normally. This experiment was carried out by the U.S. Navy, as part of their research into future uses of plastics.

On the other hand, perhaps the world will see a return to more traditional materials.

Appendix: Plastics and their uses

Common name	other names	uses
ABS	Acrylonitrile/butadiene/styrene copolymer	telephones, power tool casings, car dashboards, food mixer casings
Acetal	Polyacetal, Polyoxymethylene	gears, faucet bodies, door fittings, locks
Acrylic	Poly(methylmethacrylate), PMMA, Perspex, Diakon	aircraft cockpit canopies, faucet tops, lenses, light fittings, bathtubs, glazing panels, car rear light lenses
Acrylonitrile/vinyl acetate copolymer	Acrilan	textile fiber
Celluloid	Cellulose nitrate	ping-pong balls
Cellulose (regenerated)		textile fibers (Cuprammonium rayon, viscose rayon), cellophane
Cellulose acetate	*Cellulose ethanoate*	photographic and other kinds of thin film, acetate rayon fibers, small tool handles, eyeglasses, varnishes
Cellulose tri-acetate		textile fibers (Tricel, Arnel), motion picture film base
Epoxy resins*		adhesives, electrical insulators, surface coatings, chemically resistant paints, printed circuits
EVA	Ethylene/vinyl acetate copolymer, Alkathene	record player turntable mats, food containers, ice cube molds, WC pan connectors
Melamine-formaldehyde*	MF, Melamine-methanal, Melamine	table mats, trays, melamine worktops
Neoprene	Poly(chloroprene)	oil-resistant hoses and gaskets
Nylons	Polyamides	gear wheels, bearings, curtain rail fittings, power tool casings, nuts and bolts, zip fasteners, textile fibers
PET	Polyethylene terephthalate	polyester fibers (Terylene), polyester film (e.g. for recording tape), bottles
Phenol-formaldehyde*	PF, *Phenol-methanal*, Bakelite, Phenolic	electrical fittings and casings, pan handles, bottle tops, toilet seats, Formica worktops

Names shown in italics are the standard names laid down by the International Union of Pure and Applied Chemistry (IVPAC)

Polyacrylonitrile	*Poly(propenonitrile)*	"acrylic" textile fibers (e.g. Orlon, Courtelle), manufacture of carbon fibers
Polycarbonates		riot shields, vandalproof glazing, safety helmets, babies' bottles, computer parts, street lamp covers
Polyester (see PET)		
Polyester resins*		polyester glass-reinforced plastics (GRP), for making such things as car bodies and boat hulls
Polyimides		gears, bushes, panels, high-temperature insulators, tough flame-resistant film, rigid foams for aerospace structures
Polypropylene	*Poly(propene)*	beer bottle crates, shoe heels, packaging film, chairs, pipes, textile fibers (e.g. Nypel, Cournova)
Polystyrene	*Poly(phenylethene)*	yogurt cartons, model construction kits, disposable syringes, insulation, ceiling tiles
Polyethythene		**high density:** bleach bottles, milk crates, packaging film, **low density:** detergent bottles, cold water pipes, plastic bags, packaging film
Polyurethanes*		rigid and flexible foams, elastomeric fibers for stretch fabrics (e.g. Lycra, Vyrene), paints and varnishes
Polyvinyl acetate	PVA, *Poly(ethenyl ethanoate)*	emulsion paints, chewing gum, greaseproof paper
PTFE	Polytetrafluoro-ethylene, Teflon, Fluon	nonstick coatings, dry bearings, plumbers' tape and other sealing materials
PVC	Polyvinyl chloride, *Poly(chloroethene)*	pipes, gutters, phonograph records, curtain rails, plastic-coated fabric, floor coverings, electric cable insulation
SBR	Styrene/butadiene rubber	car tires, hoses, shoe soles, waterproof boots
Silicones		silicone rubbers, fluids (used in polishes, paints and as waterproofing agents, oils and greases) and solid resins used as electrical insulating varnishes and water-repellant, nonstick surfaces
Urea-formaldehyde*	VF, *Urea-methanal*	electrical fittings, bottle caps, toilet sets
Vinyl chloride/vinyl acetate copolymer	*Chlorethene/ethanyl ethanoate copolymer*	as for PVC

*Thermosetting plastic

Glossary

Atom The basic unit of matter that cannot, under normal conditions, be divided. The smallest part of any element that can take part in a chemical reaction.
Calendering Using a series of rollers to squeeze softened plastic into a thin film.
Camphor A white, crystalline, organic chemical that can be obtained from the wood of the camphor tree.
Carbon The element that forms the basis of all organic chemicals. The molecules of such chemicals contain carbon atoms bonded to atoms of other elements.
Catalyst A chemical that speeds up a chemical reaction without itself taking part in the reaction.
Copolymer A polymer formed from two or more monomers, each of which can independantly form its own polymer.
Dip-coating Covering an object with a skin of plastic by dipping it into molten plastic.
Distillation Separating a liquid mixture into its component parts by boiling the liquid and allowing the components to condense separately.
Elastomer A polymer with elastic properties.
Electrostatic Concerned with static electricity – electricity that does not flow but remains still (static) as a positive or negative charge on the surface of an object.
Extrusion Shaping a softened plastic by forcing it through a hole.
Fraction One of the component products that result from the distillation of crude oil.
Injection molding Forming a solid object by injecting molten plastic into a mold.
Insulation 1. Using a material to prevent or reduce heat loss, usually by trapping still air. 2. Using a material that does not conduct electricity to isolate wires and other electrical conductors from their surroundings.
Molecule Two or more atoms, of the same or different elements, joined together by chemical bonds.
Monomer A chemical with relatively small molecules that can be made to link up in long chains to form a polymer.
Organic chemical A chemical whose molecules are based on carbon atoms – like those in living organisms.
Polymer A chemical whose molecules are made up of long chains of repeating sub-units, or monomers.
Polymerization The process of causing one or more monomers to form a polymer or copolymer.
Resin 1. Any one of several solid and semi-solid polymers produced as sap by certain plants. 2. A plastic, particularly in its "raw" state, before it has been treated with plasticizers, fillers, colors and other chemicals.
Shrink wrapping A method of enclosing a product in a thin film of plastic that clings tightly to the surface.
Synthetic Artificial; man-made.
Thermosetting plastic A plastic that, once formed, only sets harder when heated.
Thermosoftening plastic A plastic that always becomes soft and pliable when heated.
Vaccum forming Shaping a thermosoftening plastic by using suction to draw a softened sheet onto a mold.

Index

ABS 35
acetate rayon 23
acrylic 17, 24, 31, 40
adhesives 30
aramids 42
asbestos 36
atoms 10

Bakelite 9, 19, 36
blow molding 20
building industry 26
bulletproof glazing 24
butadiene 32

calendering 21, 25
carbon 7, 10, 11, 12, 36
celluloid 8
cellulose nitrate 8
Chardonnet silk 22
coatings 28
compound 10
compression molding 20
copolymer 34
corrosion 6, 28
cuprammonium 22

dampproof membrane 25

elastomer 42
electrical insulators 6, 9, 27
epoxy resin 19, 29, 31
ethylene 11, 12, 17
EVA 34
expanded polystyrene 27
extrusion 20, 24

fibers 22
film industry 9
fluon 13
fractionating 16

glass-reinforced plastic 36, 39
glues 30

hydrogen 11
hydrogen chloride 13

ICI 38
injection molding 20, 26
insulation 27
isoprene 32

laminating 36
long chain molecules 18

methane gas 11
molecules 7, 11, 12
monomer 12, 31
molding 7

naphtha 17
natural gas 17, 42
nylon 13, 16, 18, 23, 36, 39

oil 16, 42
organic chemicals 16

paints 29
Parkesine 8
Perspex 13, 24, 39
plant resin 7

pollution 40
polycarbonate 18, 24, 39
polyester 13, 23
  resin 36
polyethylene 13, 17, 18, 25,
  29 38, 40
polymerization 12, 13, 19, 31, 34
polypropylene 23, 39
polystyrene 17, 18
polyurethane 13, 19, 23, 26
PTFE 13, 18
PVC 13, 17, 18, 24, 29, 39

recycling 40
resins 7
rotational molding 21
rubber 32

SBR 33
silicone 34
solvents 30
sorbothane 42
space shuttles 42
styrene 33

teflon 13
thermoplastic resin 30
thermosetting resin 18, 27, 29, 36
thermosoftening 18

urea-formaldehyde 27, 31, 35

vacuum forming 20

waste disposal 40

47

Picture acknowledgments

The author and publishers would like to thank the following for allowing their illustrations to be reproduced in this book: Paul Brierley 27, 30 (both); The Design Council 7, 13; ESPI 6, 8 (left), 9, 19 (both), 34, 35 (left); Michael Freeman *frontispiece*, 8 (right), 10, 23, 33, 35 (right), 38 (left), 42, 43; GSF Picture Library 41; Brian Hawkes 40; ICI Plastics *cover*, 17 (both), 24, 25 (bottom), 38 (right), 39; Topham 22 (top), 32; Malcolm S. Walker 11, 12, 13 (top), 14, 16, 18, 20–21, 36, 44–5; Wimpey Laboratories 25 (top), 26.

© Copyright 1987 Wayland (Publishers) Ltd
61 Western Road, Hove, East Sussex
BN3 1JD, England